Crossroads

Ellie Black

Presentation by *BookLeaf Publishing*

Web: www.bookleafpub.com

E-mail: info@bookleafpub.com

ISBN: 978-93-95784-57-3

First edition 2022

Himself

You disappeared out of my life like so many others before and I wonder what did I do? Where did I go wrong? Is my heart too full of love and longing for you that it was heavy a burden for you? I guess I will never know. You disappear out of my life and I learn to not to be a part of your life.

Unanswered questions

This rollercoaster is erratic, sporadic, so
unpredictable
Will you stay Will you go? I just don't know!
Up and down, in and out, round and about
Actions and words conflicted for sure
Really wish I could show you the door
Your actions have me on the floor
 My heart is filled with longing and sorrow
Maybe it will be better tomorrow
Or maybe not?

Me

Self kindness is what you need in order to
succeed, a lesson hard learned and long overdue
after all of this it's time to focus on you. The you
that you have yet to become now you are not
looking after everyone

Unfinished

The world is a mess but I'm
Glad you're in it.

Lost hope

5

Hope eternal
Crushed in seconds
When will it be my turn
sadness envelopes me suddenly
Tears come and then go
The dream is slowly fading away

If

If there is freedom why do we fight?
If there is darkness why is there light?
If there is lie, why do we die?
If there is truth, why do we lie?

If there is love, why do we hate?
Why do we leave everything to fate?
If there is peace why is there war?
Why is there killing from door to door?

Love conquers all, hate should disappear
There should be laughter with no more tears,
people should be happy there should be no more
hate, we have to try and stop it before it is too
late.

Do you ever?

Do you ever feel lovely?
Do you ever feel sad?
Do you ever feel cheerful?
Do you ever feel glad?

If you feel lonely
You're not the only one
If you feel sad
Try and have some fun

If you feel cheerful
Try and stay that way
If you feel glad
Keep sadness at bay

The real me

Although I've had friends all my life
They never ever see
The sadness lurking in my eyes
Wishing I was free
Although they were so close
They felt so far apart
I want to be happy to love with all my heart
Laughter is the emotion I had behind to prevent
them seeing the truth, I hope that people will
realise soon I hate all the pretence,but words fail
to pass my lips
I paste a smile onto my face and set out to
deceive I know that no one will ever know the
real me. I know that is the way it's meant to be
so I keep on lying and deep inside a part of me is
very slowly dying.

Life

Life can be very hard and painful
When all you need is peace
Situations surrounding you refuse to resolve
Depression looms like thunder
Threatening to erupt and take you to that place
where love is an unknown entity
Life is real and once around
No theory all of practice
Personalities interchange and link
To make the world different
Refuse to let despair covet you,
Reign free, project yourself

Love

What is love? A fire in your heart so powerful
no hose can disintegrate,
A hunger deep inside no food can compensate,
belonging to one person together as are one.
Without them you are bereft.

Wishing

Love is something that escapes me
Like sand falling from my hands
Like water trickling from a fountain
Love is like precious jewel
In awe of all its beauty, but never captured. A
candle in the wind so powerful yet so fragile and
the flame has gone. To love and be loved, the
precious gift of all, a true miracle that I wish on
me to fall.

Change

Change is a powerful force that completely takes
over
It gently creeps up on you until it's too late,
To turn back to the person you were, because
you are not that person anymore
In a short space of time your entire world spins;
on your ideas, thoughts and views resulting in a
renewal of your persona and the person you
were is no more.

Questions

Change is everlasting
Important to the core
Images of importance
Seem insignificant now
Values and beliefs are in question
What to believe?
The need to believe overrides my own mind
Why confide in religion based on what
evidence?
More so believe in the power of mankind and
the search for inner peace. Why delude myself
with what's expected of me? When what I search
for goes far beyond religion and delves deeper
into every aspect of my existence.

My place

A place so familiar
Now as alien as ever
Where is my place?
Where do I belong now?
In someone's arms?
I'm sure not there!
In this world of confusion
I seek sanity, a safe haven
Why is it so cruelly ripped from my hands, my
heart?
So many questions beseech me like tiny tortured
souls
Logic has left my world incomplete puzzles
remain
The never ending question
Where is my place now?

Loneliness

Loneliness my cursed friend
The constant companion
Who knows my secrets, my fears,
Loneliness the uninvited guest
Forcing the changes in me
Always in the background
Coercing me to turn around my life
The ever looming darkness threatens to erupt, to
hold me forever in the pits of its despair

Untitled

Beyond description
Beyond endurance
Distorted images
Broken dreams
For what? Some disillusionment

The grip of realism declines still a world of
fantasy reigns
Escapism such an easy tool to use, refuse to face
the inevitable
Why run from your destiny
Hold firm, be strong
Keep running and there will be nowhere left to
run

Me

Fighting against all odds
Urgent, grasping, seeking the return to the place
that I know
Expectations from afar seen believable realistic
and true
In an ideal world,
maybe. All too soon though they change as they
tend to do,the familiarities once known
disappear frantic searches do not recover them
If all becomes clear that change although
disconcerting is good but mostly essential. As a
person I have changed too. Priorities have
changed focus, change is beyond my control this
I must accept.

guarded

Strong so strong
Always and forever
Redolent to change
Must be especially now

Love torn, fractured
Yet hopeful all the same
The hard can heal, the heart takes bit longer

Slow slowly is the key
Credit to myself indeed
Keep barrier firmly in place
Until it's right.